THE FOOTBALL FRIEND'S

LITTLE INSTRUCTION BOOK

A Boyfriend's Little Instruction Book

Caleb March

B□XTREE

First published 2000 by Boxtree

an imprint of Macmillan Publishers Ltd, 25 Eccleston Place, London SW1W 9NF, Basingstoke and Oxford

www.macmillan.co.uk

Associated companies throughout the world

ISBN 0 7522 1808 5

1 3 5 7 9 8 6 4 2

A CIP catalogue record for this book is available from the British Library.

Designed by Nigel Davies. Printed by Caledonian

Illustrations by Sue Clarke

Do you think an offer of coffee automatically means sex? That Clitoris is a Greek island? Or that 'commitment' means you should be committed to lots of women? Then *The Boyfriends Little Instruction Book* will be bought by your partner and pointedly thrust at you. If you've ever wondered what the other half think – then you probably aren't even listening right now.

But if you want to know why women love shoes, little boxes, puppies and cushions, then take this book out of your sleeve and go pay for it – because they will prosecute.

The Boyfriend's Little Instruction Book is fun, fat-free and contains no cellulite, genetically modified concepts or the words 'millennium-compliant'.

The three magic words are,
'You've lost weight'.

Guilt is a great reminder
to give more presents.

Commitment is
somewhere between
six weeks and when
she divorces you.

There's a fine line between
seeing a lot of each other and stalking.

Pet names are best saved for pets.

Drive your girlfriend wild in bed.
Crap in her pyjamas.

Be good on commitment. That doesn't
mean being committed to a lot of girls.

Be polite to your
girlfriend's dad.
One day he might be
paying for the wedding.

Infatuation has boundaries:
often defined by the county court.

Your presence does not count
as a present.

Study her
Chinese horoscope,
but don't tell her if
she's a dog or a pig.

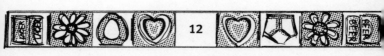

Cultivate a sense
of humour – but no gags
about nuns, fat girls
or dead puppies.

Always communicate –
as long as your parents
are paying the phone bill.

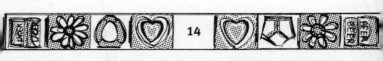

Always kiss on a first date:
you might not
get another chance.

Nicknames. If she calls
you 'stalky' there's a problem.

Also 'floppy', 'halfwit' or 'brother'.

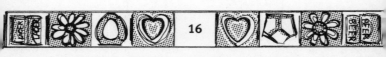

An offer of coffee
does not automatically imply sex.

Love is blind,
so look for short-sighted women.

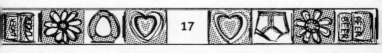

Be nice to your girlfriend's
parents; that doesn't mean
sleep with her mum.

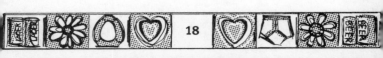

Be good in bed:
go straight to sleep
and don't snore.

A girl agreeing to
go out with you
doesn't mean you just hired
a cook and cleaner.

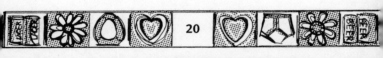

What if desperation
was attractive?

Always tell your girlfriend you love her,
even when you've done nothing wrong.

Definition of a boyfriend:
10 stone of drooling lust with acne.

Nothing says 'I love you' like a ring.
So call her occasionally.

When you're in love,
the songs on the radio are all about you.

A girlfriend is an investment: she'll show
interest and sometimes she'll go down.

Declarations of love
are fine, but not sprayed
in six-foot high letters
on a railway bridge.

The perfect girlfriend:
supports your team, makes love
as if her life depended on it
and wears nothing but
a rucksack full of chilled lager.

Send her love letters,
but remember that one day
they'll be read back to you
as evidence.

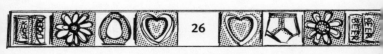

Always overtip when you're
with your girlfriend.
But not with foreign coins,
old sweets or pocket fluff.

Treat your girlfriend
like your home.
Keep her warm, well decorated
and stocked with drink.

Learn some new skills.
Talking and chewing gum
at the same time
isn't enough.

Be jealous and possessive.
Everyone *is* trying to take her
away from you.

Befriend her ugly friends:
it's safer than having them as enemies.

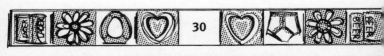

Take your girlfriend to
romantic places.
Your bedroom or car doesn't count.

The first one to say 'I love you'
doesn't automatically lose.

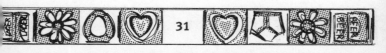

Always row on a Sunday,
so then at least you've had
the best of the weekend.

Tell her she looks great in denim,
but the material you prefer her in is 'skin'.

If she tells you she's 'late', the correct
response is not to change your name.

Don't get your girl's name tattooed
on your arm. Just get a blank scroll
and fill in the name in biro.

'We have to talk',
means you've just
been chucked.

'It's not me –
it's you!'
does too.

Respect your partners
need for space.
Don't have her spot-welded
to your arm.

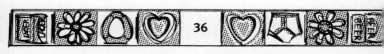

Girls love a man
in leather on a bike.
But deliver the
pizza's first.

Always phone her after the first date –
unless it's your 'one phone call'.

If she tells you that you lack
commitment, prove her wrong by
dumping your other girlfriends.

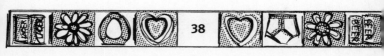

Put her on a pedestal –
especially if she's wearing a short skirt.

Flowers sent to her place of work
will always impress,
unless she's a florist.

Carve your names in a tree
(check she's not an eco-warrior first).

No matter what she tells you,
she does hate all your mates.

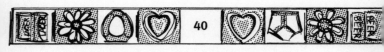

Impress your girl by taking her everywhere in a cab (not applicable to cab drivers).

Love is like the sea. Deep, restless and leaves you feeling nauseous.

Make love in the sand,
but not in a children's playground.

If she says that she loves you
like a brother, she means a monk.

Clean up your bedroom.
No woman ever got turned on by old pants,
crusty pizza and a Superman duvet.

Clitoris is not a Greek Island.

Tell her you need your 'space'. Don't tell her you mean space with other girls in it.

You don't have to spend money on presents. It just has to look like it.

It's the thought that counts.
False. It's the money.

Be faithful. If you can't be faithful,
learn to lie convincingly.

Practise saying 'she meant nothing
to me'. It'll come in handy.

Treat your girl like Cinderella. Buy her
a pumpkin and tell her it's a carriage.

Buying a girl a drink during happy hour is OK. Buying her a Happy Meal is not.

A fancy restaurant is one where the food doesn't come with the prefix 'Mc'.

Don't give nicknames to each others'
private parts. She might call you 'Mr Tiny'.

The larger the handbag,
the wider the girl.

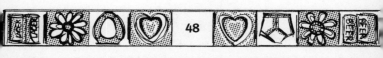

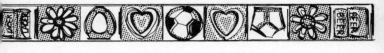

Become a Philosopher. Tell her
there's no such thing as absolute truth.

Be mature:
let her win at kiss-chase.

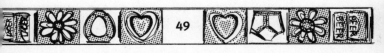

You can't make anyone
love you: not even by
standing outside her
bedroom window howling
mournfully at the moon.

Boast about your
gorgeous girlfriend to your mates,
but tell them she's mad.
You don't really want
the competition, do you?

A girlfriend can be well proportioned,
big-boned or plump, but never fat.

Never have nicer hair
than your girlfriend.

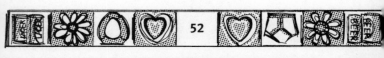

Sorry is not the hardest word. 'Croissant' and 'focaccia' are pretty difficult.

An upset girlfriend is like a computer. Crashes when you least expect it.

Redheads are fiery, brunettes are sultry, blondes have bottle.

Farting is not permitted in the first six months of any relationship.

To a woman, new shoes are like diamonds
– every angle must be inspected for flaws.

Learn about Feminism,
it makes it easier to pull the chicks.

Say 'Me too' to
anything she says –
except when she's on about
fancying George Clooney.

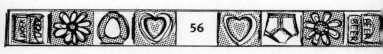

Perform tasks for her;
fight for her honour,
slay a dragon,
put up some shelving.

A girlfriend will dress to impress
for six months. Then you'll find out
what she really likes to wear
(clue: it's not what you'd
like her to wear).

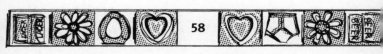

A phone conversation
with a woman is slightly longer
than with a man –
somewhere between five minutes
and FOREVER.

Treat her like royalty,
with mild disdain but
slavish devotion if she actually
comes near you.

You know it's serious
when she leaves little things
around your flat: a toothbrush,
make-up, her family.

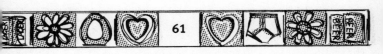

Restaurants with pictures
of the food do not impress girls.

Check for signs of unfaithfulness.
Stray hairs, different cigarettes,
men in her bed.

If she finds you in bed
with another woman, don't say
'Well, here we go again.'

Girls fancy firemen, but not you in a hard
hat and your dad's fishing waders.

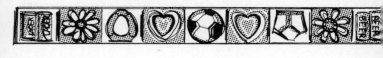

Don't offer to help her
buy clothes: your tastes
won't coincide unless
she actually is a prostitute.

Being her 'first' is a great honour –
so wait that extra five minutes
before you rush down to the pub to
tell your mates.

Cultivate flaws and bad habits.
It gives her something to talk about
to her friends.

If another man looks possessively at your
girlfriend, first make sure it's not her dad.

If you love her, set her free.
You shouldn't be keeping her
chained up anyway.

Go for short, dumpy, plain women.
They try harder.

Girlfriends are like buses.
Nothing for months, then three at once.

Girls look sexy in your shirt or sweater,
but not in your Y-fronts.

If she thinks a blowjob
is a hurricane, you're in trouble.

If you think she doesn't love you,
then she probably doesn't.

Make love
in the afternoons.
That way you won't
miss the good telly.

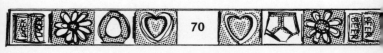

Women's preferred
lovemaking position is
with someone
financially solvent.

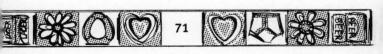

French kissing
has nothing to do
with garlic
and Gauloises.

Tear out her heart
with both your hands...
or just forget
her birthday.

If she tells you you're
belligerent and confrontational,
don't argue the point.

Be her E-male.

Don't heat your apartment:
tell her that body heat is enough.

Knowing how to unfasten
any kind of bra does not count
as mechanical knowledge.

Three reasons not to have a girlfriend.
You can fart, you can hog the duvet
and there's no one around
to see you crying, 'I'm so lonely'.

Lend her your clothes.
Better make it your
old clothes, as you won't
see them again.

Confound her expectations
by sometimes putting down
the toilet seat lid.

Treat 'I'm not in the mood' as a challenge,
unless the mood she's in is murderous.

She does have a sense of humour –
otherwise she wouldn't
be going out with you.

What she says and what she means are
two different things. Request subtitles.

For some reason
it's OK for her to wear
your clothes but not for you
to wear hers. Still, they weren't
your colour anyway.

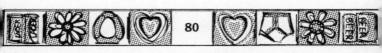

If she demands sex
at the start of the match,
she's testing your allegiances.
Give in, but don't do it
right there on the terraces.

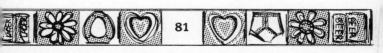

Never forget
Valentine's day or she will
be your ickle sweetums
bunnykins no more.

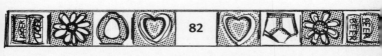

Listen to her. No, really listen to her.
You still aren't, are you?

Nothing is fair in either love or war.

Bad dumping
opener No.1:
'You know your sister…?'

Bad dumping
opener No.2:
'Remember that rash...?'

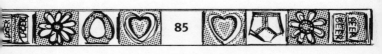

Be a good listener.
Or just get good at nodding,
smiling and going 'uh huh'.

Try moving your eyes
up to her face occasionally.

Buy her leather and rubber.
That way if she chucks you, you'll still have
material for an interesting sofa.

Vary your lovemaking positions.
Those casualty nurses like a good laugh.

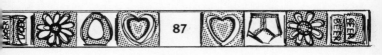

If your girlfriend and your barmaid
don't understand you, try your wife.

Just once, say to her:
'No, I'm not pleased to see you.
This is a gun in my pocket.'

Help out around the flat –
by going to the pub.

Don't get competitive
about how many partners you've had:
you're both lying anyway.

Never talk about
ex-girlfriends.
If you do, make out
they were all related
to Quasimodo.

If you're nice to her
she'll find you boring.
If you're a bastard,
she'll dump you.
I don't know the answer to this.

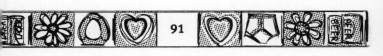

Be kind, considerate, wonderful.
Do all this before she realises
your true personality.

You can never call her too often.
Unless she's a receptionist for a major firm.

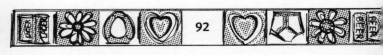

The correct form of address to
her parents is not: 'Hello. I'm the one
shagging your daughter.'

Give her a photo of you to cherish.
Not the CCTV one off Crimewatch.

Pay attention to the
little details.
Is she upset?
Does she cry a lot?
Did she leave six months ago?

Take her to Paris
at least once.
When she sees how rude
the French are,
she won't want to go again.

Diamonds are forever –
but if you don't think
it's going to last then
any shiny object will do.

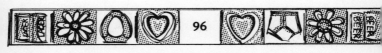

Endlessly retell the story
of how you met as if it
were the most interesting thing
in the world.

Be nice to her father.
He may own a shotgun.

When she gazes deep
into your eyes, this is not an invite
to a staring competition.

By all means buy her roses
but one day she'll say
'You never buy me roses anymore'.

The meal doesn't count
as foreplay.

When your girlfriend
insists on 'communication',
that means she wants you
to talk about her for a change.

Double date with a poorer,
less attractive couple.
By the end of the evening,
she'll be grateful she has you.

Imitation flowers
= Imitation love.

Use her feelings of insecurity and
low self-esteem against her.

There is only
lust at first sight.

There is no such thing as
a trial separation.

Take her for granted.
You're still not
paying attention are you?

'No' means no.
It can also mean maybe.
Welcome to female logic.

Women mature
more quickly
than men do:
counter this by appealing
constantly to her inner child.

Try to get her
interested
in your hobbies:
cars, drink,
masturbation.

Promise to kiss
every inch of her body.
Don't worry.
You'll only get halfway down
before you're making love.

Try to avoid 'Date' movies.
The male lead will be
more handsome, richer and
much better behaved
than you'll ever be.

Make love like a celebrity.
Imagine you're doing it with yourself.

There is never a 'right time'
to get pregnant.

Tease her during sex.
Not by saying 'I think the condoms split'.

Money can't buy you love,
but it can rent it at reasonable rates.

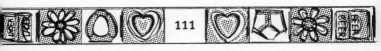

Placing a TV in the bedroom
is a sure indicator that
the sex has gone out of
the relationship.

Women often make
unsuitable clothing decisions.
When she does, don't point
and laugh at the wedding dress.

Be a sexual athlete but stop short
of doing a lap of honour.

If you like horror stories with a twist –
read her diary.

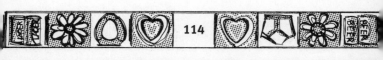

Don't be afraid of commitment.
Even Peter Pan had his Wendy.

The lady always comes first.
You know what I mean.

You're in love if
you find her irritating laugh cute,
her filthy bedroom 'cool'
and her criminal record
'characterful'.

Once you've ground away
her personality and reduced
your girlfriend to zombie-like
obeisance then it's time to ...
pop the question.

Never trust anyone
who keeps their eyes open
when kissing. Of course,
to know this you'll have to
keep your eyes open as well.

If you feel the
relationship dwindling –
book a holiday.
That will be
sure to end it.

If your relationship is
difficult and heartbreaking,
remember –
you'll never be let down
by alcohol.

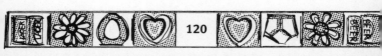

Don't just have sex in bed.
Try other places.
But be careful they don't
throw you out of the
furniture showroom.

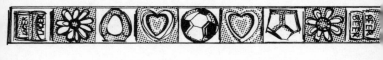

Don't introduce her
to your family.
If she wanted to visit a
shallow gene pool, she would have
gone to Norfolk.

How to tell your girl's moved in.
The bedroom's a boudoir,
the bathroom's a chemical plant
and you've moved mentally
to the pub.

Half-hearted
suicide attempts
will rarely bring a woman
running back.

To have loved and lost
is better than
never to have loved at all.
Yeah, right!

When all else fails,
be a grown-up and
accept the blame.
It might get you a final shag.

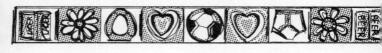

Caleb March has been described as a lover, Lothario and loser by so many of his 'insignificant others' that we can no longer ignore it. A professional cad, he was schooled at Bromley and Belmarsh before going on to Cambridge, which he described as 'a smashing day out'. Rapidly becoming a man of the world, March soon learnt to place women on a pedalo. Among his numerous partners, there have been some that are real.

He dislikes liver, the Tuba, the word 'slacks' and has been known to wear a cravat. He considers the art of swallowing oysters to be 'practise for the ladies'. Among his many hobbies are speed-cribbage, drum'n'bass and hanging around Airport Arrivals lounges with a sign reading: 'Anyone?' He often refers to himself in the third person and his only regret is being unable to locate the self-help section in bookshops.